Nicole Petrick

Current Questionnaire Generation Tools - A Market and P

Nicole Petrick

Current Questionnaire Generation Tools - A Market and Product Overview

GRIN Verlag

Bibliografische Information der Deutschen Nationalbibliothek: Die Deutsche Bibliothek verzeichnet diese Publikation in der Deutschen Nationalbibliografie; detaillierte bibliografische Daten sind im Internet über http://dnb.d-nb.de/ abrufbar.

1. Auflage 2006
Copyright © 2006 GRIN Verlag
http://www.grin.com/
Druck und Bindung: Books on Demand GmbH, Norderstedt Germany
ISBN 978-3-640-39411-1

CURRENT QUESTIONNAIRE GENERATION TOOLS – A MARKET AND PRODUCT OVERVIEW

by

Nicole Petrick

Master of Economics and Management Sciences Programm
Wirtschaftswissenschaftliche Fakultät
Humboldt-Universität zu Berlin

Seminar: E-Business Case Studies

Institut für Wirtschaftsinformatik

Wintersemester 2005/06

Berlin, February 28, 2006

ABSTRACT

The paper mainly focuses on current questionnaire generation tools on the German-speaking market. Additionally, an introduction to internet-based research is given in Part One of this paper that will explain the differences between online surveys and online experiments and the choices of when and when not to conduct an experiment on the internet. It will also shortly introduce advantages and disadvantages of online research as well as the current standards that have been derived so far.

Part Two of the paper gives a short market analysis on the market of questionnaire generation tools with its suppliers and demanders, explaining the past and current development of the market as well as its future trend.

The main focus lies on the product analysis in Part Three. Comparative features that will be looked upon when analyzing different products will be derived from the standards, introduced in Part One of this paper. A choice of current suppliers and their products will be represented and the positioning of their products within the market explained. Two favored products are then compared in more detail according to features, usability and pricing scheme, presenting a short result from the comparison thereafter.

A summary will be given at the end that will recapitulate the results from the paper.

TABLE OF CONTENTS

I. INTRODUCTION 1

II. INTERNET-BASED RESEARCH – AN INTRODUCTION 2

    1.   INTERNET-BASED RESEARCH PROJECTS 2
        i.   *Online Surveys* *3*
        ii.   *Online Experiments* *3*
    2.   THE CHOICE OF WHEN TO CONDUCT AN EXPERIMENT ONLINE 4
    3.   ADVANTAGES AND DISADVANTAGES OF ONLINE RESEARCH 4
    4.   STANDARDS FOR ONLINE RESEARCH 5

III. MARKET ANALYSIS 8

    1.   PAST MARKET DEVELOPMENT 8
    2.   CURRENT MARKET STATE 9
        i.   *Supply side* *9*
        ii.   *Demand side* *10*
    3.   TRENDS 11

IV. PRODUCT ANALYSIS 13

    1.   COMPARATIVE FEATURES 13
    2.   CURRENT SUPPLIERS AND THEIR PRODUCTS 15
    3.   ANALYZING PERFORMANCE VIA SCORE POINTS 21
    4.   PRODUCT POSITIONING.. 24
    5.   GLOBALPARK VERSUS ASK4MORE – A COMPARISON 25
        a.   *Features*... *25*
        b.   *Usability*... *26*
        c.   *Pricing scheme* *28*
        d.   *Outcome*.. *29*

V. SUMMARY... 30

APPENDIX.. 31

REFERENCES.. 35

ii
LIST OF TABLES

Table 1: Evaluated Products..14

Table 2.1: Technical features...16

Table 2.2: Technical features...17

Table 3: Business features..18

LIST OF ILLUSTRATIONS

Figure 1: Results of score points per level of functionality....................................20

Figure 2: Results of overall score points compared with maximum........................21

Figure 3: Portfolio map of product positioning...22

Figure 4: ask4more's GUI (trial version)...25

Figure 5: Globalpark's GUI (demo version)...25

LIST OF ABBREVEATIONS

ADM   Arbeitskreis Deutscher Markt- und Sozialforschungsinstitute e.V.
[Working Circle of German Market- and Social Research Institutes]

ASI   Arbeitsgemeinschaft sozialwissenschaftlicher Institute e.V.
[Working group of social-scientific Institutes]

BVM   Berufsverband Deutscher Markt- und Sozialforscher e.V.
[Association of German Market- and Social Researchers]

DGOF   Deutsche Gesellschaft für Online-Forschung e.V. (D.G.O.F.)
[German Society for Online Research]

NEON   Network Online Research

OSS   Online Survey System

EITO   European Information Technology Observatory

ICT   Information and Communication Technology

GUI   Graphical User Interface

VAT   Value Added Tax

I. INTRODUCTION

Adapting to Stephen W. Hawking's illustrative metaphor of the universe put into a nutshell[1], one could envision the world encrypted into the internet. There is nothing in the real world, where its interactive counterpart could not be found in the endless network of the World Wide Web – may it be obvious or hidden. Despite the early stages of the internet's preceding forms in the 1970s, today's internet especially experienced a tremendously fast development during the last decade, becoming a medium of the masses for the masses. User statistics are constantly rising and even if, in the early stages, the internet user was in average of higher education, English speaking and male, he is now a counterpart of the inhabitant of the real word. The internet is a medium for everybody. Statistics[2] show an ever growing participation. Of course, there are still demographic deviations from the real-world counterpart. However, considering the German-speaking regions of Germany, Austria and Switzerland only, demography and social status hardly differ, thus making the region quite homogenous. Data[3] for Germany subsequently estimates a high current digital media universe of over 55% of the current population, with an active digital media usage of about 39%, where females account for 41%, teenagers below the age of 18 represent about 10% and people of 55 years of age or older, account for 14.5% of all internet users. As a consequence, the reason for social scientists and marketing researchers to discover the internet as a new research medium is quite obvious.

Online-Research in the German-speaking region still has a young but already moving history behind. It started off with simple HTML-programming and continued, accordingly to the overall technical development, to derive standards and rules for quality, reliability and validity. A new market developed, providing software tools for the development of online surveys and experiments due to more complex programming languages. The main characteristic of the new market: lacking transparency.

---

[1] See Hawkings, S. (2004): Das Universum in der Nussschale. dtv.

[2] See Nielsen//NetRatings (2002): Europäische Internet Nutzung Januar 2002.

[3] See Nielsen//NetRatings: NetView Usage Metrics: (January 2006)
http://www.nielsen-netratings.com/news.jsp?section=dat_to&country=ge (Home Panel, Web Usage Data)

II. INTERNET-BASED RESEARCH – AN INTRODUCTION

1. Internet-based research projects

In the beginning of the mid-nineties of the 20th century, using the World Wide Web as a method of research was the choice of only a small number of first movers among experimental researchers. Ten years later "we are in the midst of an Internet revolution in experimental research" (Reips, 2002a, p.243). However, what does "internet-based research" mean? To begin with, it is important to mention that several terms are used simultaneously: web research, online research, internet research, web-based research, World Wide Web research. Historically, as for the example of the term "web experiments", the term "web" was the first term used. On the other hand, the terms "internet-based research" or "internet-based experiments" do also include internet services such as e-mail, telnet, ftp or messengers for communication (e.g. ICQ, MSN Messenger) that are no web services as such due to their definition and functionality. What this paper focuses on, is research done in the World Wide Web via a web browser using the web as the underlying tool. However, due to the fact that many authors use the term "online" for describing the above mentioned version of research, this paper will adapt this term analogously. In the further paper "online research", "online surveys" and "online experiments" will thus refer to research, surveys or experiments conducted in the World Wide Web using the web with the help of a web browser.

The history of online research is strongly tied with the development and success of the internet. Attributable to the development of the number of internet users, the critical mass, necessary to conduct experiments in order to achieve a validity that coincides with the sociography and demography of the real world, was reached[4]. Due to the fact that research objects could now be recruited in a large amount within a short time, in order to be interviewed and from which to derive data, the entrance barriers for professional and empirical research sank and allowed research within a wider range. Subsequently, the internet and especially the World Wide Web with all its occurring

---

[4] See Introduction of this paper.

social processes did not only become the subject of research, but a research method itself.

As mentioned before, online research can be conducted in different ways. According to Reips[5], there are three main possibilities to collect data online that will allow conclusions to be drawn on the behavior of humans: none-reactive data collection, online surveys and online experiments. The last two mentioned will be looked upon further.

i. Online Surveys

Online Surveys, as none-experimental methods, are the most commonly used technique for online research. They are not only used by research institutes for professional, empirical research but mostly by market researchers or online-marketing experts. Surveys are an every-day fly by when surfing the internet, either as pop-ups, via e-mail or posted on a website in an either plain HTML or using Java script and Flash. Their purpose is defined as a "systematic gathering of information from respondents for the purpose of understanding and/or predicting some aspect of the behavior of the population of interest" (Tull, 1993). The frequent use of surveys is explained by the "ease" with that they can be "constructed, conducted, and evaluated" (Reips 2002b, p.230). This ease, however, still needs to be looked upon in the preceding parts of this paper. Moreover, online surveys do not necessarily need to have a scientific background; they mostly have a commercial one. However, especially for validity there are rules and standards to be considered that apply to surveys as well as to other forms of online research such as experiments.

ii. Online Experiments

According to Reips, online experiments have an advantage over online surveys or other methods of data collection via the internet, "because of their ability in proving causal relationships between variables" (Reips 2002b, p.229). Online experiments are the new and third from of experiments, that existed as laboratory and field experiments

---

[5] See Reips, U.-D. (2002): Theory and techniques of Web experimenting.

already before. They are seen as a mixture of the both predecessors, however neither taking place in a laboratory nor within a real field. Online experiments are based upon the use of multimedia technology and are conducted within the World Wide Web. The main aspect of research currently done on online experiments focuses on their validity and on the avoidance of errors as well as the derivation of standards and special techniques.

2. The choice of when to conduct an experiment online

There are several reasons, why the internet may be a good setting for an experiment to be conducted[6]. The speed with which it can be done, the low costs that arise, the high degree of automation and a wider sample are just some of the reasons that support the use of online experiments and online surveys. Online research, however, is still not reaching everybody in the world and even if the average internet-user is not too far off the average person of the real-world society, it is still mostly depending on the kind of sub-sample that is to be reached whether the internet can give representative results. Additionally, online experiments, more than online surveys, are not the most suitable method for all kinds of research projects. Its borders are the ways of measurement: the only answers that can be retrieved are those that were given voluntarily by the user; the only questions to be asked are those that can be mutually understood within the range of the possibilities of the web. On the one hand, experiments can not apply physical tests (touching, feeling, tasting). On the other hand, participants can not be controlled in their seriousness, commitment and verity with which they participate and answer. The experimental outline and the target group set the limitations of whether an online research project can replace the former real-world approaches.

3. Advantages and Disadvantages of online research

The ease of access to a large number of potential participants that are both demographically and culturally diverse is one of the mayor advantages of online

---

[6] See Part II.3. of this paper.

research. Additionally, researchers argue that "rare and specific participant populations" (Schmidt, 1997)[7], for instance drug dealers, can be reached. The advantages and disadvantages that will be mentioned here were carefully derived and listed by Ulf-Dietrich Reips[8], resulting in eighteen advantages countering seven disadvantages, while each disadvantage was directly accompanied by a solution. Next to the already mentioned advantages and the avoidance of time constraints, organizational problems and high costs, online research comes by with the ease of acquisition of participants and the ease of access for participants. Experimenter effects and demand characteristics can be reduced, while a greater external validity due to greater technical variance and a better generalization of the findings can be achieved. Additionally, motivational confounding can be detected while a public control ensures the observance of ethical standards. However, high voluntary participation endangers self-selection and multiple submissions to occur. Furthermore, the reduced or lacking interaction with the participants may lead to misunderstanding and thus creates problems for the participants to answer questions correctly. The lack of control over participants in addition leads to dropouts. All of the above endanger the quality of data and thus its validity. The external validity of online experiments, on the other hand, may also be limited due to the dependence on the technique in use.

4. Standards for online research

As aforementioned, current research on online experimental design focuses on its validity and on the avoidance of errors as well as the derivation of standards and special techniques. The foreword of the German Society for Online Research (D.G.O.F), given in a book on online research[9], presents a harsh but realistic comment on the quality of the current state:

Nicht alles, was sich heute "Online-Forschung" nennt, genügt den Ansprüchen, die zu Recht an seriöse und qualitative hochwertige Forschung gestellt werden. Und zwar

---

[7] As quoted by Reips (2002a)

[8] See Reips, U.-D. (2002a): Standards for Internet-Based Experimenting. Experimental Psychology, 49 (4), 243-256

[9] See: Welker, M, Werner, A. And Scholz, J. (2005): Online-Research. Markt- und Sozialforschung im Internet.

unabhängig davon, ob es sich nun um akademische oder anwendungsbezogene Online-Forschung handelt. (Deutschen Gesellschaft für Online-Forschung (D.G.O.F.) e.V.)[10]

Quality dimensions are generally difficult to determine, nevertheless, their importance for online research is constantly rising. Standards and rules to ensure the quality of online surveys were already derived in 2000 and 2001 by the DGOF, the ADM, the ASI and BVM[11]. However, these rules and standards concentrate more on ethical and juridical aspects or on the general action of carrying out online surveys. NEON, the communication platform for institutional and business online market researchers[12], derived requirements that software for online questionnaires should meet[13]. These requirements are quite extensive but lack the explanation of why and from where they were derived. Additionally, they coincide with most requirements, derived by Reips[14]. Consequently, this paper will focus on the sixteen standards for online experimenting that were introduced by Ulf-Dietrich Reips and will use them to develop the features for the comparison of software products in the preceding Part of this paper. These standards are a summarization of what needs to be remembered and what should be used as a "standards-check-list" (Reips, 2002a) when not only conducting an online experiment but also when conducting online surveys. According to Reips,

Internet-based experimenting is fast becoming a standard method and therefore it is a method that needs standards. [...] Without established standards the likelihood is high for making grave errors that would result in loss or reduced quality of data, in biased results, or in breach of ethical practices. (Reips 2002a, p.254)

Interestingly, the first standard mentioned is the one to "use a web-based software tool to create [...] experimental materials" (Reips 2002a, p.254). These tools are supposed to have advantages, since they automatically (should) implement standard procedures that can avoid problems otherwise occuring. This paper consequently focuses on the standards that can be used as features for questionnaire generation tools in order to

---

[10] Approximated English meaning: Not everything that is called "online research", meets the demands, rightly put to serious and qualitatively high research, not depending whether it is academic or use-oriented online research.

[11] See http://www.adm-ev.de. See List of Abbreviations for Details.

[12] See http://newweb.bvm.org/Ueber-NEON_83_0_0.html.

[13] See NEON Network Online Research (2003): Anforderungen an Online-Umfragesoftware. Entwurf einer Checkliste für NEON/BVM.

[14] See Reips, U.-D. (2002a): Standards for Internet-Based Experimenting. Experimental Psychology, 49 (4), 243-256

see whether current software suppliers do meet the state of the art on research that is currently done and that will still proceed to even further needs and requirements.

III. MARKET ANALYSIS

1. Past market development

The market of software, providing tools for online research, is strongly tied with the development of online research on the one hand and programming languages as well as the overall technical development of the IT world on the other. In the beginning and for several years thereafter, web researchers were programming their materials and procedures themselves, using the quite simple language of HTML. With enough knowledge on the language, and on the services and structures provided in the internet, conducting online research was only moderately complicated. However, programming languages developed further, web pages do now appear in XHTML or PHP, use Java Script and more recently even Flash to attract interest. Researchers hardly want or can acquire these new technical skills, thus setting the demand for applications that provide tools in order to program more complex websites without needing to code by hand.

Additionally, online research has a moving development behind. In the end of the 20th century, many research institutes evolved, providing research for the masses online. With the rise of the "new economy", online research vividly spread, as did online research institutes. After the "new economy's" fall, many new and small research institutes disappeared again, however, due to rising numbers of internet users, online research continued to develop. As the well-established, traditional research institutes (e.g. Infratest, GfK) adopted online research into their portfolio; most remaining online research institutes changed their core competencies towards either also providing offline research, towards specializing on certain topics or towards providing software solutions – questionnaire generation tools.

2. Current market state

i. Supply side

It is quite difficult to set up a kind of "state of the art" report on the current market state on questionnaire generation tools. When using Google's search tool[15], the search term <questionnaire generation tool> for pages in German only, returns 566 page hits[16]. Many pages occur multiple times; some are not current and most have the search terms somewhere in the text but not in the combination given. This result is mostly dissatisfying. When searching for <"questionnaire generation tool">, again for pages in German only, only 7 hits are returned. Thus, searching the tools required needs multiple combinations of search terms, in either English (questionnaire generation software, questionnaire software, questionnaire tool, online survey) or German (Umfragegenerator, Online Umfrage, Online Umfrage Software...) as either single search terms or as a stringent combination. The term <Online Umfrage Software> returns 2.800.000 hits, which is also the combination returning qualitative pages that are appropriate in order to find software suppliers for the German-speaking market. One splendid hit returned was that of the company "SoftGuide"[17]. This page returns a current market overview on software for market researchers, market research, surveys, web surveys and survey software. SoftGuide claims to be up-to-date (January 2006) with an overall of over 7.500 products of about 5.200 suppliers, producers and service providers in their database. However, the ranking of the software listed on SoftGuide does not coincide with the top hits of the Google web search. It is not clear, whether SoftGuide uses a criterion to develop a ranking and of what kind it could be. Besides, the information on the site is not retrieved by research but relies on the willingness of suppliers to provide information and to list their solutions on SoftGuide's side. As for the commercial suppliers, the German-speaking area lists 33 suppliers of

---

[15] See http://www.google.de

[16] All data retrieved on February 15, 2006.

[17] See http://www.softguide.de/software/marktforschung.htm

questionnaire generation tools. Another valid source, having an overview on companies and freelancers supplying online surveys is "marketing-börse"[18]. The online portal, which is giving suppliers of marketing services a place to present themselves, lists 51 suppliers for online surveys but only 5 different companies when looking for products.

None of the sources found were able to supply a market listing that can satisfy completeness. The current market is neither transparent nor at a state that is supplying reliable information. From all the research conducted, the assumption lies near that the supply side of software tools to generate questionnaires is neither large nor actively communicating or marketing their products. The market is still in a young state – most companies exist only since five years, only few supply their products for longer, at the most for ten years. A key factor, indicating a small overall market size is the non-existence of large, well-known software companies within the market. If the cake would be a big one, then large companies would surely try to get a piece of it.

ii. Demand side

The reason, why the market of questionnaire generation tools is rather a small one, is given when looking at the demand side. Demanders for online research are mostly institutes, who supply their own software solution, professional or semi-professional researchers, who use non-commercial software or renounce excessive high-tech programming and marketing researchers. The last group, predominantly working for companies, is the only one that is a demander for high-tech and high-price software solutions that can provide all standards and the ability to code the newest programming languages. Consequently, the market is small with only few demanders, who are willing to pay high prices for software solutions, thus neither leading to a highly profitable small market nor to an overall large market size.

---

[18] See http://www.marketing-boerse.de

3. Trends

EITO's[19] current press release introduced a positive forecast in respect to the growth of the European ICT market in 2006. The market for information and communication technology (ICT) is forecasted to show an average growth of 3.2 %, while the market will benefit from the "relative strength of the IT services and software sectors." The software market is expected to increase by 5.7%; however, system and network management as well as storage and security software are expected to be the main contributors to the growth in this sub-sector. Trends for a tremendous growth of the market size for questionnaire generation tools are thus not widely foreseeable, mostly due to the limited range of demanders. However, new research areas for online research, such as the 360°-analysis or 360°-feedback on employees questioning and the costumer contentment analysis will lead to a higher demand for companies, thus leading to a further development of surveys and to growth for certain suppliers. Further specialization as well as consolidation, especially between larger institutes (example of Infratest and Emnid), are trends that are quite obvious. Globalpark GmbH, a supplier of a software solution, which is at least in the number of employees[20] claiming to be a market leader, stated a growth rate of 60% for the last year[21]. This fact, combined with a rather small overall market growth, indicates a further consolidation also within the group of suppliers. As a result, the market will develop towards a market with some leading and some specialized suppliers. Lacking transparency will diminish with the large amount of small companies that characterize the market today. Specialization and consolidation is the trend, most probable leading to a consistent but rather small overall market growth. As for now, online research can be considered "revolutionär für die Marktforschung"[22] (Welker/Werner/Scholz, 2005) that brought many movements into the area of empirical research within which it surely will not loose of any

---

[19] See http://www.eito.com

[20] 50 employees

[21] All data retrieved through telephone interview with Marcel Bruder, Client Development Manager, Globalpark GmbH (February 24, 2006)

[22] Approximated English meaning: revolutionary for market research

importance. Instead, continuing to push online research towards higher quality, reliability and validity will induce further gains of importance even for many different fields of research – social, psychological and marketing. According to the ADM "Online-Befragungen werden in der Markt- und Sozialforschung als Technik der Datenerhebung in den nächsten Jahren erheblich an Bedeutung gewinnen."[23]

---

[23] Approximated English meaning: Online surveys will considerably gain on importance in market and social research within the next years.

IV. PRODUCT ANALYSIS

1. Comparative features

Demands towards software that is supposed to supply support for certain tasks to be done, are most certainly not limited. However, it is of high importance to define the requirements and features that will make a distinction between good software and weak one. There are four levels of functionality that are to be distinguished[24]:

(1) Erection and generation of the questionnaires
(2) Test functions [e.g. pretests]
(3) Server functions [e.g. user management] and
(4) Evaluation functions.

The basic functionality thereof is the first: the erection and generation of the questionnaire, which itself is being differentiated again into two levels:

(1.1) questions and question types and
(1.2) layout.

Accordingly, the standards for online research, as derived by Reips, will be considered accordingly in order to define the features and requirements the software should provide or fulfill. As for the *(1) Erection and generation of the questionnaires*, the following standards and requirements should be satisfied: Firstly, the software should provide the possibility to program in different languages. The advantages of non-HTML scripting languages and plug-ins may outweigh their disadvantages. However, this should be a case to case decision, also depending on the length of the experiment and the sub-sample that is to be reached. The software therefore should satisfy pure HTML needs as well as more sophisticated programming of XHTML or PHP and also allow Flash or Java Script to be implemented. As for the layout, a full customization that allows a corporate design to be implemented, as well as the application on the current

---

[24] See Wecker/Werner/Scholz 2005, p. 21

status with the help of a progress scale, should be possible. In order to influence time and degree of dropout, the warm-up and high-hurdle techniques have to be allowed to be implemented. Accordingly, the software should allow different levels of questions to be asked at any time. This does not only mean that personal information and motivational confounding can be retrieved at the beginning, this also implements the possibility of using higher solutions or layouts in the beginning in order to influence loading times. Other functions include filter questions that are of high importance. The software thus should be able to apply a filter to any question within the questionnaire. Furthermore, it should be possible to randomize questions and to choose whether a question is optional or requires an answer. In order to ensure the security of personal information and to avoid external access to protected directories or other intrusion, the software should automatically avoid obvious naming of files, folders, field names and conditions.

Also, the software should supply *(2) Test functions.* This implies the check for configuration errors[25] as well as the check for consistency. Configuration errors, erroneous filter questions or inappropriate answer options should be checked within the pretest of the survey. Consistency checks, instead, should detect inappropriate or erroneous answers while the experiment or survey is running and currently being answered by a participant. The quality of data can also be ensured, if the software is able to exclude data sets, which do not meet certain criteria, automatically. Additionally, in order to avoid multiple submissions, the software should either use technical measures to collect information e.g. about the IP-address of the participant or allow the implementation of password-dependent access.

Moreover, but nonetheless also of high importance, are those features concerning *(3) Server functions* and *(4) Evaluation functions.* Experiment log and other data files should be kept for later analyses and experimental materials should be kept available on the internet. User or address management can be of importance if user data was retrieved, to be re-used for future experiments or surveys. Helpful is also an existing invitation management. The evaluation, however, is of even higher significance. Next

---

[25] See Reips 2002a, p.252

to the analysis of answers and reactions retrieved, also dropout should be reported and analyzed. In order to make erroneous answers applicable, a time-stamp should be given to any answered data set. As for the evaluation, statistics should be generated in table form as well as graphically and should be available for export in either raw form (CSV) or directly into statistical programs such as SPSS, Microsoft Office Excel or other statistic programs. Moreover, the *usability* will be looked upon. This includes the general ease of use of the product, whether it has a graphical user interface, implements a wizard, has a help function or even supplies direct support of any kind.

Furthermore, to all of the above technical features that will be looked upon, some *business features* will also be considered. It is of importance whether the product is a commercial or non-commercial product and whether it is of open source or proprietary. The overall product price and possible additional services available are the final features to be examined.

2. Current suppliers and their products

As already aforementioned, lacking transparency is the mayor obstacle for an analysis to be conducted on the market of questionnaire generation tools. Subsequently, a measure needed to be implemented in order to decide on whether a company should be included or disclosed from the product analysis. Therefore, the results from the "Google" web-search[26] were used as a first estimate. Only hits on the first three pages were included for a further research. Additionally, companies were included according to their appearance within topic-related literature, either online (e.g. within online portals or online-papers) or offline (e.g. books, newspapers). Thus, a company's level of public representation was tried to be derived and used as a measure.

Moreover, the sample was chosen in a way as to supply the widest range of products currently available. Hence, in addition to the commercial and rather sophisticated products, three non-commercial and to a certain extent simple products were included.

---

[26] See Part III.2.i of this paper.

Furthermore, in alignment with the reference to online experiments, the current version of Wextor, developed by Reips and Neuhaus, was also included in the analysis.

The below table lists all the companies with their products that were examined. A reference ID was given, which will be used in all further tables. Additionally to the company's name, the product name and current version is listed. Also, it can be seen whether the product is client- or web-based and whether the generated survey will be automatically hosted or not.

Table 1: Evaluated Products

ID	Company	Product	Version	Type	Hosting
1	ask4more	ask4server	4.0	web-based[27]	no[28]
2	Chris Hübsch, TU Chemnitz	Xquest	2.3a	client-based	no
3	egrade	egrade Professional Edition	3.7	client-based	no
4	Globalpark	umfragecenter	4.0	web-based	yes
5	IfALT	Popollog	-	web-based	yes
6	Inworks GmbH	inquery Survey Server	7.4	web-based[29]	no[30]
7	ISI GmbH	EQUIP® Questionnaire Generator	2006	client-based	optional[31]
8	NetQuestionnaires	NetQuestionnaires Enterprise Edition	5.7	web-based[32]	no[33]
9	Paul Marx-Marketing Consulting	eQuestionnaire Business	2.5	web-based	yes
10	Reips& Neuhaus	Wextor	2.4	web-based	no
11	Rogator Software AG	Rogator G	4	client-based	optional[34]
12	Wendland& Berger	Q-Generator	1.1	web-based	no

---

[27] Integrated into the client's intra- or extranet

[28] Due to installation on client's server, ask4server is not hosted by ask4more. All other versions are hosted.

[29] Installation on client's server.

[30] Due to installation on client's server, Inworks' inquery Survey Server is not hosted by Inworks.

[31] Depending on Version – online (CAWI) or offline (CAPI).

[32] Installation on client's server.

[33] Due to installation on client's server, NetQuestionnaires' Enterprise Edition is not hosted by NetQuetionnaires.

[34] Hosting software available for installation on own server.

All companies supply the client with software in the pure sense – the program either needs to be installed on the client's computer system or on the client's server. Exceptions are "Popollog", "eQuestionnaire" and "Q-Generator" that are purely web-based, just like "Wextor", which is a "web-based tool for generating and visualizing experimental designs and procedures" (Reips and Neuhaus, 2002). Additionally, "eQuestionnaire" is representing an online survey system (OSS). However, all companies emphasize the developed software as the underlying tool or even have the development of the software as their core business activity. This is the reason why amundis communications GmbH's "2ask"[35] was not included. Despite the fact, that "2ask" is also an OSS; the company emphasizes rather the services around the tool than the tool itself. The software is also not available separately but only within the OSS.

The following table shows the first part of the technical evaluation of the products. The erection and generation of the questionnaire as well as test functions were evaluated. The erection and generation was not only divided into the aforementioned levels of "layout" and "questions and question types" but listed as "layout", "question types" and "functions". "Layout" thus refers to the code with which the questionnaire is generated and also gives information about the customization possibility and whether the progress scale is applicable. "Question types" refers to all common question types, which includes the existence of radio buttons, check boxes, drop-down menus, free numerical entry fields, free text entry fields and the possibility to establish matrix questions. "Functions" includes the option of applying filters to questions, to choose whether a question is optional and to see whether the correctness of an answer is checked (e.g. whole number, within a range). Test functions refers to the possibility of pre-testing, whether the software performs consistency checks while the questionnaire is running and whether multiple submissions can be avoided and time stamps are given. The table lists all the required features if the questionnaire generation tool incorporated them. Thus, the more features listed, the better. However, a tool can not

---

[35] See http://www.2ask.de

list more features then the ones that were checked. The maximum possible number of features derived in Part IV.1 of this paper is given in the complete features' checklist[36].

Table 2.1: Technical features

ID	Erection and Generation			Test Functions
	Layout	Question types	Functions	
1	PHP, customization of design, progress scale	all common, rankings, one-question-one-page	Filter questions, answer check, optional answer, randomization	Pre-test, consistency check, multiple submission avoidance, restricted users
2	HTML, PHP	all common, grouping of questions with Java script possible	no program but configuration scripts for xslt-processors	Multiple submission avoidance or user restrictions via TAN, time stamp
3	PHP, ASP, Java script, customization	all common, one-question-one-page	Filter questions, answer check, optional answers	Pre-test
4	HTML, Java script, customization, progress scale	all common, constant-sum-scales, rankings, one-question-one-page	Filter questions, answer checks, optional answers, randomization	Pretest, consistency checks, time stamp
5	HTML, configuration as defined in NFILE and VFILE	As defined in AFILE and WFILE, one-page-all-questions	As defined in RFILE	Multiple submission avoidance via IP address/ browser configuration check and cookie placement
6	HTML, Java script, customization, progress scale	all common, one-question-one-page	Filter questions, answer checks, optional answer	Consistency check, multiple submission avoidance, user restrictions
7	HTML, customization	all common, constant-sum-scales, rankings, image map, graphical scale, one-question-one-page	Filter questions, answer checks, randomization, optional answers, time control	Consistency check, time stamp
8	HTML, customization, progress scale	all common, dynamical questions, one-page-one-question	Filter questions, answer checks	Pre-test, multiple submission avoidance, user restrictions via password

---

[36] See Appendix.

ID	Erection and Generation			Test Functions
	Layout	Question types	Functions	
9	PHP, customization, progress percentage	all common, one-question-one-page	Filter questions, answer checks, randomization, optional answers	Time stamp
10	HTML, Java script	all common, one-question-one-page	Automatic high-hurdle technique	Multiple submission avoidance via user ID, time stamp
11	HTML, Java script, customizing, progress scale	all common, graphical scale, one-question-one-page	Filter questions, answer checks, randomization, optional answer, time control	none
12	Generates plain HTML code	all common w/o matrix questions, one-page-all-questions	none	none

Table 2.2 shows the second part of the technical assessment, including the server and evaluation functions as well as the results from the usability check. Server functions include possible user, address or invitation management that is additionally offered next to the generation and hosting of the questionnaire. This feature does automatically not apply for client-based products. Evaluation functions imply all possibilities to evaluate the received answers, whether can be done per table or graphically as well as if and how a data export is possible. Usability then proves whether help functions, a wizard or even support is supplied.

Table 2.2: Technical features

ID	Server Functions	Evaluation Functions	Usability
1	Invitation management	Permanent analysis per table and graphical, export as CSV, to SPSS, MS Excel,	Online-help
2	none	Mean and deviation, Export to CSV	Only for sophisticated users with knowledge of HTML, XML, PSP, MySQL, no GUI
3	none	Results as list, graphical analysis, supports group evaluation, export as CSV, copy&paste to Excel	Wizard, Help-function, Online-help
4	Invitation management	Permanent analysis, graphical analysis, export as CSV, to SPSS, dropout	Help handbook, electronic central library, support per mail and telephone

ID	Server Functions	Evaluation Functions	Usability
5	Generation of FIN-list (identification numbers), publication within registered users	Data export as pdf, rtf, tex, png, CSV at any time	Knowledge about CSV configuration text files necessary
6	Invitation management (within software)	Permanent analysis per table and graphical, export to SPSS, MS Excel	Help function
7	none	Permanent analysis per table and graphical, Export as CSV, to SPSS, dropout	Help function
8	none	Permanent analysis per table and graphical, export as pdf, to SPSS, MS Excel	Support
9	none	Permanent table analysis, export to MS Excel and SPSS, dropout	Support forum
10	none	none	Short online help
11	none	Permanent analysis per table and graphical, export to SPSS, MS Excel, Quantum, Triple S, dropout	Hotline support
12	none	none	Help via e-mail contact possible

The evaluated business features are listed in the following Table 3. The table gives information on the software model as well as on the business model. It is examined whether the software is free, open source or proprietary and whether the product itself is of commercial or non-commercial kind. Additional services that are available are listed and the price for the evaluated product (without additional services) is given.

Table 3: Business features

ID	Software model	Business model	Additional Services	Price in EUR[37]
1	proprietary	commercial	Customizing, System introduction, training	10.000,-[38]
2	open source	non-commercial	none	free
3	proprietary	commercial	Consulting, hosting, result analysis, training, workshops	899,-
4	proprietary	commercial	training	1.000 – 100.000 (depending on use)[39]

[37] All prices without value added tax.

[38] For basis module and installation, not including travel costs for installation. Additional costs EUR 300 for each concurrent user. Additional costs for pocket-pc-module: EUR 350 per licence.

[39] Prices vary depending on number of interviews and whether a project- or a permanent license is purchased. Prices according to telephone interview with Marcel Bruder, Client Development Manager, Globalpark GmbH (February 24, 2006)

ID	Software model	Business model	Additional Services	Price in EUR[40]
5	proprietary	non-commercial	none	free
6	proprietary	commercial	Full-service	8.850[41]
7	proprietary	commercial	Training, generation and realization of surveys, hosting on client's server	individual[42]
8	proprietary	commercial	Full-service, training, customizing software for client's need	16.999[43]
9	proprietary	commercial	none	385,- (per year)[44]
10	proprietary	non-commercial	none	free[45]
11	proprietary	commercial	Software introduction, training, consulting Interviews, e-mailing, Full-service online survey/analysis, Panel access	individual[46]
12	proprietary	non-commercial	none	Free

All features where derived with the help of the information given on the web pages of the companies' products and by personal evaluation. Most products were evaluated with the help of trial versions or free test accounts. Additional information, which was not possible to retrieve with the above methods, was collected by directly contacting the company via e-mail or per telephone.

3. Analyzing performance via score points

In order to be able to analyze the given results from the table further, a graphical analysis was conducted. Therefore, to each feature a score point was assigned, while assigning score points to the overall product when the software implemented a feature[47]. On the whole, 22 points were distributed, plus three additional points. Additional points were assigned to enhanced question types that are not necessarily needed but enable an even more sophisticated questioning while opening new

---

[40] All prices without value added tax.

[41] Module system. Elementary module, installed on client's server: EUR 8.850.

[42] See Appendix

[43] Excluded are costs for installation, included is one training (10 persons). Additional annual costs: EUR 3.400.

[44] Prices for business users. Prices differ for students and universities.

[45] Donations via PayPal possible.

[46] See Appendix.

[47] See Appendix for complete feature list with score points.

possibilities to the range of questions asked. These include graphical scales, image maps and dynamic questions. The score points were aggregated according to the levels of functionality, while the erection and generation of the questionnaire was evaluated on the three sub-levels from the table analysis. The evaluation was conduced on the product basis, thus not comparing each product on the level of functionality but comparing the overall product performances with each other.

Figure 1 shows the results from the score point analysis of each product, listing the results on the basis of each level of functionality.

Figure 1: Results of score points per level of functionality

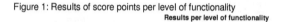

Results per level of functionality

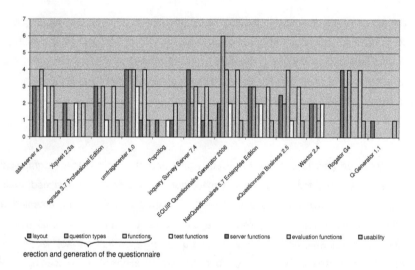

| □ layout | □ question types | □ functions, | □ test functions | ■ server functions | □ evaluation functions | □ usability |

erection and generation of the questionnaire

The maximum number of points per level is as follows: four points each were assigned to layout, question types and functions, thus leading to an overall of twelve points for the erection and generation of the questionnaire. Furthermore, four points were assigned to test functions and evaluation functions, server functions as well as usability were equally assigned with one point each. Thus, the maximum for each scale in the above graphic is either one or four points. However, question types implements a possibility to receive an additional of three points, thus leading to a maximum of seven points. Note that the EQUIP Questionnaire Generator 2006 reached six points in that field. Figure 1 already visualizes the strengths and weaknesses of the products in a whole. While most products score high in the question types and evaluation functions, weaknesses occur concerning test functions. Additionally, it can be seen that server functions are often lacking, whereas usability is mostly given.

Additionally, all score points were aggregated and compared to the maximum number of possible scores in order to better visualize the overall performance of a single product. As a result, Figure 2 shows how well a product performed and how far it is still away from the ideal point.

Figure 2: Results of overall score points compared with maximum

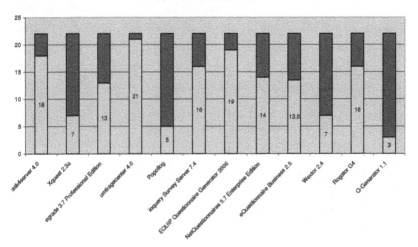

Results show that all commercial products scored higher than the non-commercial ones. Surprisingly, also Wextor 2.4, the tool developed by Reips and Neuhaus, does score low. Globalpark's umfragecenter 4.0 is the clear favorite, scoring 21 out of 22 points and thus meeting almost all requirements. ISI GmbH's EQUIP® Questionnaire Generator 2006, as a client-based product, scores second-best, followed by ask4more's ask4server 4.0. As a result, a clear correlation between the performance of a product and its price can be seen. Moreover, there is no relationship between the performance of a product and its type – whether client- or web-based. The overall result is an intermediate one, with few strong products and few weak products. The majority of all commercial products scored an average of 16 points. This implies that standards, especially the ones known as the NEON criteria, are widely met. However, the standards and requirements that are supposed to ensure a better validity and quality of data – those standards derived by Reips – are not yet widely met. A further improvement on this field needs to be done.

4. Product positioning

The examined sample of products was willingly chosen in a way as to reflect a wider range of what currently exists in the market of questionnaire generation tools. However, due to the additional choice of products according to the result of the "Google" web-search, the sample may already slightly represent the market. Therefore, a portfolio map was established. Within the portfolio analysis, the product character (commercial / non-commercial) and the product type (client-based / web-based) was compared. Furthermore, the price was included, indicated by the size of the bubble. Figure 3 shows the results of the analysis.

Figure 3: Portfolio map of product positioning

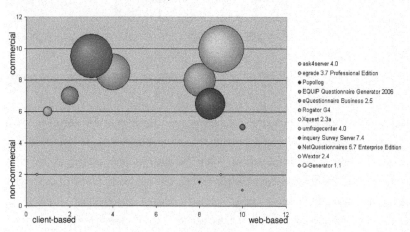

Products were compared according to the product character and type on a 10-point-scale. The exact number, however, does not have any significance. Actually, both characteristics are of a 0/1-type, the scale was enlarged in order to allow a graphical conversion. Because the size of bubbles represents the price, all free products were set on a price of EUR 100 in order to make them visible.

The above figure shows that products rather tend to be web-based than client-based. Non-commercial products are mostly web-based, while commercial products are almost equally distributed between both types. Moreover, there is no significant price variation between client-based commercial products and web-based commercial products. Hitherto, it needs to be mentioned that most companies with client-based products, which were examined in this paper, also offer web-based versions. Thus, the overall impression that current questionnaire generation tools are rather web-based than client-based, can be approved.

5. Globalpark versus ask4more – a comparison

Two questionnaire generation tools will now be evaluated in more detail. As a result from the analysis, Globalpark's umfragecenter 4.0 will be compared with ask4more's ask4server 4.0. Both products are web-based, scored high in the features' analysis and are equally positioned within the market, while located in a high-price segment. Consequently, ask4more and Globalpark are direct competitors[48].

a. Features

It was quite noticeable that Globalpark scored extremely high in the later score point analysis, based on the table analysis. Thus, the features will be listed again in more detail and comparatively. The web-based questionnaire generation tool "umfragecenter 4.0" generates a HTML code as well as Java script, the layout of the questionnaire is fully customizable, while a graphical progress scale can be implemented. "ask4server" equally allows full customization and a graphical progress scale to be put into service. However, ask4server 4.0 generates the questionnaire in PHP only. This does not need to be a disadvantage for the questionnaire in use, yet, multiple options for the

---

[48] Even though ask4server is not hosted, ask4more still offers other licences that are also hosted.

programming language, including HTML, was based as reference. Both products apply all common question types plus rankings and allow a one-question-one-page design. Though, only umfragecenter 4.0 also supports constant-sum-scales. Filter questions, , the randomization of questions and answer checks and the choice of whether a question should be optional or stringent are features to be found in both questionnaire generation tools. Additionally, umfragecenter 4.0 supports dynamical questions and even loops to be generated. Both products then lack one feature in the level of test functions. While ask4server 4.0 does not implement time stamps, no reference towards an avoidance of multi submissions was found when analyzing the features of umfragecenter 4.0. Nonetheless, both products supply a pre-test, as well as consistency checks. In addition, both support an invitation management as well as a permanent table and graphical analysis of the data retrieved, which also can be exported at any time given as CSV to SPSS or other statistical programs. However, only umfragecenter 4.0 also gives an analysis on the dropout rate and returns the page with the highest dropout.

A few words need to be said on the character of pre-tests. Most products' pre-test simply consists of the generation of the questionnaire that then can be manually tested by going through the questionnaire. Umfragecenter 4.0 generates pre-test with the software running through the survey while randomly generating answers for a given number of times, followed by the test result and a test statistic. The tested ask4more version, did not implement this first-class test type. Ask4server 4.0, however, is offered with a similar pre-test under "live conditions".

b. Usability

Both products come with a user-friendly graphical user interface (GUI). Ask4more's software solution is rather browser orientated; Globalpark, on the other hand, put a GUI in a quite typical client-based software solution look into action. Nevertheless, both versions are well-structured and easy to understand. From all products tested, umfragecenter 4.0 and ask4more's trial version ranked best for "ease of use". The below screen-shots show the trial version of ask4more's questionnaire generation tool, as well as the demo version of Globalpark's umfragecenter 4.0.

Figure 4: ask4more's GUI (trial version)

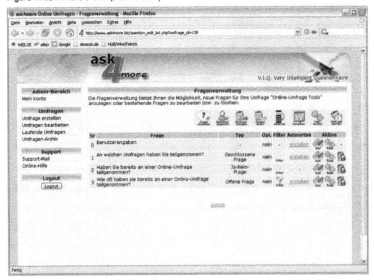

Figure 5: Globalpark's GUI (demo version)

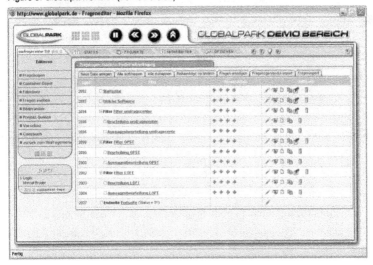

c. Pricing scheme

Both companies have a quite complex pricing scheme, adapting their prices to the client's demand. Thus, different licenses are available. Actually, most questionnaire generation tools are offered with either project license or time license. Time licenses usually allow an indefinite number of projects to be conducted as well as a large number of interviews, if not even indefinite. Project licenses vary in either the number of projects to be conducted or the number of interviews per project. On the other hand, client-based software solutions are sold for a fixed price but may be discounted or even for free if an additional online license, which includes hosting, is purchased. Most companies still manage to keep the pricing scheme in a quite simple way or to make it at least fit a one-page-format, others do not. Unfortunately, Globalpark is a company of the latter. Its price range comprises prices from EUR 1.000 up to EUR 100.000. Prices vary depending on whether a permanent or project license is purchased and on the level of use – the number of interviews to be conducted. Ask4more, on the other hand, belongs to the former group, announcing their pricing policy already on their website. Next to the free trial version ask4free, a starter version (ask4starter), a university version (ask4student) and a business version (ask4business) are available, while prices are directly announced. The above models vary with the number of projects and the number of interviews per project that can be conducted. The server version, with an unlimited time frame as well as unlimited projects and interviews, consequently has a more complex pricing system. The basis module, with one user account (administrator) has a price of EUR 9.500 plus an additional EUR 500 for installation and configuration, not including travel costs. Each additional user account (editor) amounts to a further EUR 300 per concurrent user, leading to an overall price for one user of EUR 10.000 (excluding travel costs and VAT). As a result, prices of current questionnaire generation tools can not be compared directly due to their pricing structure. Current questionnaire generation tools prices need to be applied to the certain demand and requirement of the client, in order to make a comparison possible.

d. Outcome

Considering functionality only, Globalpark's umfragecenter 4.0 is the unambiguous favorite. However, ask4more's ask4server is still a good quality product, underlying a continuous further development that hopefully leads, in the near future, to an equally satisfying result within a similar analysis as conducted above. As for the decision of when or when not to conduct online research, the choice of what product to prefer needs to be adjusted to the personal requirements and needs. Of course, for validity and data quality Globalpark's umfragecenter 4.0 is currently the best. Prices, however, might in the end be the decisive factor for the decision of what product to put in use.

V. SUMMARY

The paper tried to give an impression on the current state of the art within the market of questionnaire generation tools. Thereby, an introduction to the current state of online research was equally given as well as an explanation on the topic itself. The later market and product analysis, conducted according to the standards and requirements that were set through research in this field, proofed the following: Firstly, the market of online research as well as the market for questionnaire generation tools are still in an early stage. However, online research is leading the development with its approach of setting standards and rules in order to ensure data quality, validity and allow generalization. The market of questionnaire generation tools yet lacks behind these requirements. However, tendencies are evidently visible that both – research and business – try to further push the development towards a high-end online research. Second, the market of questionnaire generation tools can be simple described by lacking transparency. There is a yet not strictly identified number of suppliers on the German-speaking market. Furthermore, the number of serious suppliers, those companies that both offer a sophisticated product and that will not faster disappear from the market than they appeared, is small. An estimate gives 5-10 companies on the German market that can be considered as serious. While it can be surely stated that online research will further develop and be pushed to a true scientific level, only time will show to what direction, despite the tendency to consolidate and specify, the market of questionnaire generation tools will definitely develop.

APPENDIX

Features' checklist with score points

Version: Client-/web-based: Hosted:
Price calculation: Additional services:

1. Erection and Generation of questionnaire: **(12 Points)**
    a. Layout (4 Points)
        • Languages: 2 Points (HTML = 1 + x =1)
        • Design possibilities: Customization = 1 Point
        • Progress scale: = 1 Point
    b. Questions and question types: (8 Points)
        i. What question types are possible? *(4 Points)*
            1. Radio boxes ⎤
            2. Check boxes
            3. Matrix questions
            4. Drop Down-Boxes   } Common question types = 1 Point
            5. Numerical entry fields
            6. Free text entry fields ⎦
            7. Constant-sum scales = 1 Point
            8. Rankings = 1 Point
            One-question-one-page = 1 Point

> Additional Points: dynamical questions, image map, graphical scale

        ii. Functions: *(4 Points)*
            1. Filter questions possible – for any question = 1 Point
            2. Answer checks = 1 Point
            3. Stringent answer / optional answer adjustable = 1 Point
            4. Randomising of questions = 1 Point
            5. Warm-up and High-hurdle technique possible[49]

2. Test functions: **(4 Points)**
    - Pre-tests = 1 Point
    - Consistency checks for data quality = 1 Point
    - Multiple response avoidance (IP address check / password generation) = 1 Point
    - Time stamp = 1 Point

2. Server functions: **(1 Point)**
    - Address- or invitation management = 1 Point

3. Evaluation functions: **(4 Points)**
    - Evaluation of answers:
        o Per table
        o Also graphically = 1 Point
        o While survey is still running = 1 Point
    - Dropout analysis = 1 Point
    - Export of data = 1 Point
        o CSV, SPSS, MS Excel

4. Usability: **(1 Point)**
    - Help functions, Wizard, Support

---

[49] If customization in layout is possible, then warm-up and high-hurdle technique are applicable.

Pricing model EQUIP® Questionnaire Generator:

a) Business licenses:

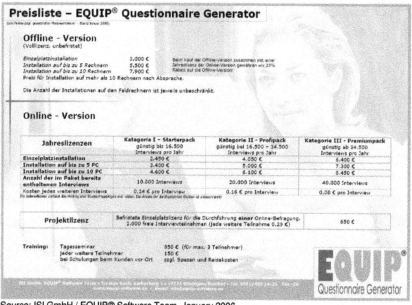

Source: ISI GmbH / EQUIP® Software Team, January 2006

b) Non-commercial license:

**Preisliste – EQUIP® Questionnaire Generator – für Universitäten, Hochschulen, Schulen
(Stand Februar 2006)**

Online - Version

Nicht- kommerzielle (Lehr)Version
Volllizenz, unbeschränkter nicht-kommerzieller Einsatz bis zu 25 Studien pro Jahr, nur für Universitäten, Hochschulen und Schulen erhältlich
Nutzungsgebühr: € 850,- für 12 Monate

Training:	Tagesseminar	950 € (für max. 3 Teilnehmer)
	jeder weitere Teilnehmer	150 €
	bei Schulungen beim Kunden vor Ort	zzgl. Spesen und Reisekosten

Ansprechpartner: ISI GmbH/ EQUIP® Software Team, Torsten Koch, Ascherberg 2, 37124 Göttingen/Rosdorf.
Tel. 0049 551 489 74 25, Internet: www.equip-software.de Email: info@equip-software.de

Source: ISI GmbH / EQUIP® Software Team, February 2006

Pricing model Rogator Questionnaire Generator:

Rogator Preisliste Januar 2006

Zeitlizenzen	Anzahl Projekte	Freie Interviews	Hotline-Support	Euro
Zwei Jahre	unbegrenzt	50.000	8 (h)	21.900,00 €
Ein Jahr		20.000	4 (h)	11.900,00 €

Projektlizenzen (Vertragslaufzeit unbegrenzt, Projektlaufzeit max. 3 Monate)	Anzahl Projekte	Freie Interviews	Hotline-Support	Euro
Maxi	10	10.000	4 (h)	9.900,00 €
Medium	5	5.000	2 (h)	5.500,00 €
Mini	3	3.000	1 (h)	3.600,00 €
Projekt	1	1.000	1 (h)	1.250,00 €
Verlängerung Projektlaufzeit / Monat				350,00 €

Zusatzleistungen				
Zusätzliche Interviews	bis 500 150,00 €	bis 1.000 250,00 €	Bis 3.000 500,00 €	Bis 10.000 1.000,00 €
Email-Aussendung (pro selektierte Zielgruppe)	bis 1.000 150,00 €	bis 5.000 250,00 €	bis 15.000 500,00 €	+ 10.000 + 250,00 €

Full-Service	Wir erstellen Ihre Umfrage komplett im Full-Service	
Design	Sie liefern die Vorgaben – wir erstellen das Design als wiederverwendbares Template	300,00 €
Fragenerstellung Pro Frage	Umsetzung des Fragebogens mit der Rogator-Software	40,00 €
Umsetzung weiterer Sprachen Pro Frage	Für gängige Fremdsprachen 30,00 €	Für Fremdsprachen mit Sonderzeichen (z.B. Kyrillisch, Mandarin, Japanisch, Tschechisch) 55,00 €
Bildbearbeitung Pro Bild	Anpassen von Grafik-/Bilddateien an das Fragebogenformat, sofern diese nicht 1:1 gestellt werden	40,00 €
Korrekturen Pro Stunde	Einarbeitung nachträglicher Korrekturen 1. Stunde ohne Berechnung	125,00 €

Source: Rogator Software AG, January 2006

REFERENCES

ADM Arbeitskreis Deutscher Markt- und Sozialforschungsinstitute e.V. (2001):
Standards zur Qualitätssicherung für Online-Befragungen. [pdf]
URL: http://www.bvm.org/Richtlinien-Standards_7_0_0.html:

ADM Arbeitskreis Deutscher Markt- und Sozialforschungsinstitute e.V. (2000):
Richtlinie für Online-Befragungen. [pdf]
URL: http://www.adm-ev.de:

Beatty, P. (2004): Pretesting Questionnaires: Paradigms of cognitive interviewing
practice, and their implications for developing standards of best practice. In Prüfer,
P., M. Rexrothand F.J. Fowler, Jr. (Eds.). Quest 2003. Questionnaire Evaluation
Standards. ZUMA-Nachrichten Spezial Band 9. Mannheim. [pdf]

EITO Update 2005 - ICT market. October 2005 [pdf] URL:
http://www.eito.com/download/Presentation%20Update_PK_17_10_2005.pdf:

Gräf, L. (1999): Optimierung von WWW-Umfragen: Das Online Pretest-Studio.
URL:http://www.globalpark.de/de/mydocs/Artikel_Optimierung_www_umfragen.pdf

Grealish, D. (2004): Pretesting Questionnaires: The New Zealand Experience. In
Prüfer, P., M. Rexrothand F.J. Fowler, Jr. (Eds.). Quest 2003. Questionnaire
Evaluation Standards. ZUMA-Nachrichten Spezial Band 9. Mannheim.

Gscheidle, C. and M. Fisch (2005): Der Einfluss der Computerausstattung auf die
Internetnutzung. Ergebnisse der ARD/ZDF-Online-Studien 1997 bis 2005. [pdf]
URL: http://www.zdf.de/ZDFde/download/0,1896,2002843,00.pdf:

NEON Network Online Research (2003): Anforderungen an Online-Umfragesoftware. Entwurf einer Checkliste für NEON/BVM. [pdf] URL: http://newweb.bvm.org/user/neon/NEON-DOC-L-2.pdf:

Nielsen//NetRatings (2002): Europäische Internet Nutzung Januar 2002. [pdf] URL: http://www.nielsen-netratings.com/news.jsp?section=new_pr:

Nielsen//NetRatings (2003): Europäische Frauen im Internet. [pdf] URL: http://www.nielsen-netratings.com/news.jsp?section=new_pr:

Nielsen//NetRatings (2003): Immer mehr Silver-Surfer nutzen in Europa das Internet. [pdf] URL: http://www.nielsen-netratings.com/news.jsp?section=new_pr:

Nielsen//NetRatings (2003): In Europa nutzen derzeit knapp zwölf Millionen Kinder und Jugendliche das Internet. [pdf] URL: http://www.nielsen-netratings.com/news.jsp?section=new_pr:

Prüfer, P., M. Rexrothand F.J. Fowler, Jr. (Eds.). Quest 2003. Questionnaire Evaluation Standards. ZUMA-Nachrichten Spezial Band 9. Mannheim. [pdf]

Reips, U.-D. (2002a): Standards for Internet-based experimenting. Experimental Psychology 49 (4), 243-256.

Reips, U.-D. (2002b): Theory and techniques of Web experimenting. In Batinic, B., U.-D. Reips and M. Bosnjak (Eds.) Online Social Sciences. Hogrefe&Huber. Seattle.

Reips, U.-D. and Neuhaus, C. (2002): WEXTOR: A Web-based tool for generating and visualizing experimental designs and procedures. Behavior Research Methods, Instruments, and Computers, 34, 234-240.

SoftGuide's market overview on software for market researchers, market research, surveys, web surveys and survey software. [htm]
URL: http://www.softguide.de/software/marktforschung.htm:

Statistisches Bundesamt (2005): IKT IN DEUTSCHLAND. Informations- und Kommunikationstechnologien. Vierteljahresergebnisse. 1. Vierteljahr 2004 bis 2. Vierteljahr 2005 [pdf]
URL:http://www.destatis.de/download/d/veroe/faltblatt/broschuere_ikt04_05.pdf:

Statistisches Bundesamt (2005): Qualitätsbericht. Erhebung über die Nutzung von Informations und Kommunikationstechnologien in Unternehmen.[pdf]
URL: http://www.destatis.de/download/qualitaetsberichte/qualitaetsbericht_ikt.pdf:

Tull, D. and D. Hawkins (1993): Marketing Research - Measurement & Method, 6th Ed., New York, Macmillan.

van Eieren, B. and B. Frees (2005): Nach dem Boom: Größter Zuwachs in internetfernen Gruppen. ARD/ZDF-Online-Studie 2005. [pdf]
URL: http://www.zdf.de/ZDFde/download/0,1896,2002526,00.pdf:

Welker, M., A. Werner, A. and J. Scholz (2005): Online-Research. Markt- und Sozialforschung mit dem Internet. dpunkt.verlag

FURTHER ONLINE SOURCES

http://www.2ask.de/orbiz/DigiTrade/Business-Paket--66d.html

http://www.ask4more.biz/content/ask4server.php

http://www.huebsch-gemacht.de/programmieren/xslt/

http://www.dgof.de/dgof.php

http://www.egrade.de/

http://www.eito.com/tables.HTML

http://equestionnaire.de/

http://www.evaluieren.de/infos/links/frageboe.htm

http://ifalt.com/

http://www.inworks.de/inquery.html

http://www.psychologie.unizh.ch/sowi/Ulf/Lab/WebLabLinksD.html

http://www.softguide.de/software/marktforschung.htm

http://www.softguide.de/partner/psuche.php3?at=e&art=sws&id=sgn&anfrage=&bsy
s=alle&rubrik=C4.20&ld_ausw=alle&plz_eingabe=&hr=on

http://www.netq.de/index.cfm/fuseaction/product.server.html

http://www.nielsen-netratings.com/news.jsp?section=dat_to&country=ge

http://www.nua.com/surveys/index.cgi?f=VS&art_id=905358729&rel=true

http://www.globalpark.de/de/marktforschung/online-marktforschung/online-
marktforschung.html

http://www.zuma-webstudien.org/

http://www.popollog.de/dokumentation/index.hhtml

http://www.form-maker.de/q-generator-ge-1-1.html

http://www.equip-software.de/

http://www.rogator.de/content/cms/front_content.php?idcat=114&navmark=24

http://www.rogator.de/content/cms/upload/the_race/race.html

http://silicon.de/cpo/sguide/sget.php3?id=silicon&seite=software/marktforschung.htm

http://www.stanford.edu/group/siqss/Press_Release/press_detail.html

http://psych-wextor.unizh.ch/wextor/en/index.php

http://www.gesis.org/asi/asi1.html

http://infosoc.uni-koeln.de/wwwpretest/